Susan Fanella

W9-AKV-045

★

With WINGS LIKE Eagles

a DEVOTIONAL

★

Copyright © 1998 Thomas Kinkade,

Media Arts Group, Inc., San Jose, CA

All rights reserved. Written permission must be

secured from the publisher to use or reproduce any

part of this book, except for brief quotations

in critical reviews or articles.

Published in Nashville, Tennessee,

by Thomas Nelson, Inc., Publishers.

Unless otherwise noted, Scripture quotations are from

THE NEW KING JAMES VERSION.

Copyright © 1979, 1980, 1982, Thomas Nelson, Inc., Publishers.

Scripture quotations noted NIV are from the HOLY BIBLE:

NEW INTERNATIONAL VERSION ®.

Copyright © 1973, 1978, 1984 by International Bible Society.

Used by permission of Zondervan Publishing House. All rights reserved.

Printed in the United States of America

1 2 3 4 5 6 7 - 04 03 02 01 00 99 98

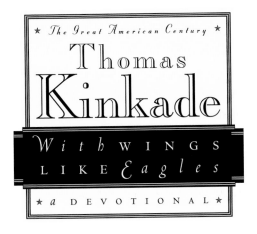

★ *The Great American Century* ★

Thomas
Kinkade

With WINGS
LIKE Eagles

★ *a* DEVOTIONAL ★

with

CALVIN MILLER

THOMAS NELSON PUBLISHERS
Nashville

A GREAT NATION

Now the LORD had said to Abram:
"Get out of your country,
From your family
And from your father's house,
To a land that I will show you.
I will make you a great nation;
I will bless you
And make your name great;
And you shall be a blessing.

GENESIS 12:1–2

These words given to Abraham might have been given to any of the founders of the American dream, for through America much of the world has been blessed. America is one of the few nations ever to become great without some driving agenda for conquest. There are some who claim that America has grown rich because of imperialism. Yet after which war did America claim to own those whom she had vanquished? To which open nation that needed betterment has she not in recent years sent Peace Corps personnel? How often has she sent boatloads of food and clothing to those who suffered from hunger and nakedness? These are not the ways of a conqueror. In every age in which people have suffered since America became a nation, America

insisted that the most important part of being human was human rights. Truly, through America, have all the nations of the world been blessed. Through her desire to end all suffering and famine, America has always been there for those who have been abused by power and cast out of their own nations into refugee camps.

America's need to see every person in the world be "better off" fueled the endless waves of immigration that beckoned the poor and disenfranchised of the world to come to her shores.

But America is not a nation created by the will of any of her past outstanding leaders. Jacques Maritain wrote in *Reflections on America*: "The great and admirable strength of America consists in this, that America is truly the American people."[1]

To understand oppression, it is necessary to have been oppressed.

The *Amistad* was a vessel owned by slave traders that, long after slave trading had been banned in the United States, was confiscated by the United States. Her cargo of slaves was brought to New England. An American ex-president and the courts of New England, through long and tedious investigations and trials, at last delivered the poor passengers of the *Amistad*, who had been captured in Africa and brought to the slavery auctions of Cuba for

illegal sales to elsewhere in the world.

Although America was slow to free her own slaves, the Amistad incident resulted in America's direct assault on the worldwide slave trade. The incident spoke to something deep in the fabric of the American philosophy. America's best export is freedom, her worldwide dream that all people should be in charge of their destiny.

God didn't ordain America to arrogantly see herself as a blessing to the world. God ordained Americans to take their blessings and publish the benediction throughout the world. Then through the people called Americans—those who had received much—would much be given. Through Americans would all the world be blessed.

P r a y e r : *Lord, it is conceit that says that all the people of the world need to be Americans. But it is honestly born in Your great heart that all people of the world have a right to Your blessings. Thank You for providing us these blessings of life, liberty, and the pursuit of happiness.* ★

The Blessings of Law

I am the LORD your God,
who brought you out of the land of Egypt,
out of the house of bondage.
You shall have no other gods before Me.

Exodus 20:2-3

America has made famous this great declaration: "I am the Lord who brought you up, You shall have no other gods before me." Nearly every county in America erected a courthouse during its formative years. Americans wanted all cities in the nation to have access to justice. These courthouses ensured every citizen the hope of being protected by the law. Innocence would prosper in these houses; guilt would meet fair play.

God gave the Ten Commandments so that all human relationships would know the safeguard of justice. The safeguards of all of our liberties is the law. It was Daniel Webster who said, "God grants liberty only to those who love it, and are always ready to guard and defend it."[2] Law is the guarantor of all that Americans would ever call liberty. Webster also said, "One country, one constitution, one destiny."[3]

Only once have I served on a jury responsible for sending a young man to prison. I will never forget that awful, tense moment after the

jury had reported and the judge had rapped the gavel. "Twenty years!" said the judge. The man seemed to deflate before our very eyes. His chest seemed to cave in. His mother began weeping. The prosecution team beamed. But it was the judge who captured my attention. He rose with a leaden demeanor. He had passed the sentence, but the judgment was not easy for him. He knew he had sentenced a young man to jail for what would be the best part of his productive years. He knew that when the young man returned home most of his friends would be gone. Many of his family would no longer be there. He would have to live for the rest of his life with the label *convict*.

Law weighs heavy offense, because without the law there is only chaos. Justice can be very costly. But who really was to blame? The criminal himself, of course.

But God understood the weight of all those commandments He handed to Moses that were much later adopted by America. And the architects of the American Dream knew what they were doing when they lettered the ancient words of the commandments in stone on the Supreme Court building.

The justice of the Ten Commandments is essential to any nation. So many nations of the world have tried to copy that affection for law

born in Exodus 20. Fukusawa Yukichi, the Japanese statesman, said, "The final purpose of all my work was to create in Japan a civilized nation as well equipped in both the arts of war and peace as those of the Western world."⁴ To be sure, America's love for the Ten Commandments has produced an utter idealism missing in so many of the tyrannical nations of the world. It was Justice Brandeis who said, "There is in most Americans some spark of idealism which can be fanned into a flame. It takes something of a divining rod to find what it is: but when found, and that means often, when disclosed to its owners, the results are often extraordinary."⁵

So it is with justice.

P r a y e r : *Lord, if our love of Your commandments has made our justice system great, what would the loss of those commandments mean? Root us further—ever further—in the idealism of Your law. Then the courthouses will be justice houses, and honor will thrive.* ★

PIONEERS

They commanded the people, saying, "When you see the ark of the covenant of the LORD your God, and the priests, the Levites, bearing it, then you shall set out from your place and go after it. Yet there shall be a space between you and it, about two thousand cubits by measure. Do not come near it, that you may know the way by which you must go, for you have not passed this way before."

JOSHUA 3:3–4

Jesus Christ is called a "pioneer" by the writer of the Book of Hebrews. This word really means "first goer." All pioneers are first goers. They go into the unknown and mark for others the safest way.

Joshua of Israel cried out, "When you see the ark of the covenant of the LORD your God, and the priests, the Levites, bearing it, then you shall set out from your place and go after it . . . that you may know the way by which you must go, for you have not passed this way before." God's church is a colony of pioneers marking the safest way to freedom.

Life would be simple if we always knew where we were going. Since we do not, we need a guide. The church has guided America through the hard times. The way into the future has always been fearsome and exhilarating. Most of us are forced to confess with Joshua, "We have never been this way before."

Amy Lowell wrote,

This is America,
This vast confused beauty,
This staring, restless speed of loveliness,
Mighty, overwhelming, crude, of all forms,
Making grandeur out of profusion,
Afraid of no incongruities,
Sublime in its audacity,
Bizarre breaker of moulds.[6]

America could not help becoming the grand international pioneer, for her citizens have all been pioneers. Her vast lands could be tamed only by pioneers. But having learned the soul of the power, she has never been selfish with the compass.

Not far from my Oklahoma birthplace is a statue called the *Pioneer Woman,* a bronze sculpture of a woman and her son. It towers on its pedestal to a height of thirty feet or so. When I was a child, we traveled what seemed a long distance to see the "biggest statue in Oklahoma." I was enthralled. My grandparents had settled

Oklahoma long before its statehood. I was a child of the prairies. To meet this great, towering statue was to encounter my heritage.

The bronze prairie queen wore a corroded grace—both the lady and her son were green. But even as a child I understood that art was a conveyor of beauty. Here in bronze was a multitoned image of a woman whose indomitable demeanor was her thirty-foot testament to the strength of a pioneer. Where was her tall bronze husband? Who could say? You knew by looking at her that she was a widow. Taming the prairies was hard, and only the scattered graveyards of the eighteenth century really tell the story.

But that woman was American. That woman was as America itself—born to tame the prairies and to build a civilization. That's what pioneers did.

Prayer: *Lord, we are the children of pioneers. Give us children the spirit of our forebears. Help us to admit when we are confused and that we need You as did our "first-going" forebears. We beg the compass of Your direction, so that we do not wander aimlessly into the future looking in vain for the paths of national greatness.* ★

F O L L O W   M Y
D E C R E E S   .   .   .
I   W I L L   N O T   A B A N D O N   Y O U

Concerning this temple which you are building,
if you walk in My statutes,
execute My judgments, keep all My commandments,
and walk in them, then I will
perform My word with you, which I spoke
to your father David. And I
will dwell among the children of Israel, and
will not forsake My people Israel.

1   K I N G S   6 : 1 2 – 1 3

God desires to stand by His people. Throughout the Bible, God stood by those who remained faithful to Him. America has always felt an obligation to defend those whose causes are right. When the people of other nations have suffered the onslaught of tyranny, Americans have felt their pain. We have sometimes become involved in war to secure their liberty. America's churches have prayed over their young men and women and with a sense of divine reluctance, have then sent their brightest and, best to liberate and defend these dispossessed.

But Americans believe that God is the real Defender of the best

of America's dreams. God is invoked in Kate Smith's rousing entreaty to ". . . Bless America." The anthem pleads for God to ". . . stand beside her and guide her, through the night with a light from above." In America God is seen as a great friend of every nation that wants to do it right. America feels some divine calling to establish liberty throughout the world.

Paul Galico's novella, *The Snow Goose*, rends the heart. A handi-capped lighthouse keeper, whose crippled condition kept him from entering the English Army in the Great War, lamented his inability to serve, yet he faithfully kept the light in his lighthouse. In the unfolding of the war, a snow goose with a broken wing came to his lighthouse. Having lost the season for migration, the bewildered bird allowed the lighthouse keeper to mend her broken wing. At last the healed goose could fly. Sadly for its healer the goose left with the next migration.

Then came Dunkirk. The English Army was trapped by the Germans on the cusp of the European mainland. The appeal went out for all who had boats to cross the Channel and bring back the soldiers who were in danger of being massacred. The lighthouse keeper at last found a way to serve his country. In his tiny boat he crossed the Channel several times, saving English soldiers from the German

assault. It was said by those he rescued that a huge, white goose flew before him in the dense smoke and fog, always pointing the way to freedom. At the end of the tale the lighthouse keeper himself was lost to the fierce waves of the Channel, but the lives he saved were many.

The implications of the story are as supernatural as they are obvious. God is the original lover of liberty, and in times of war and confusion He watches . . . *through the night with a light from above.*

The faithful dependence of all our defenders may be echoed in the Westminster Chimes:

> *Lord, through this hour, be thou our guide,*
> *So by thy power no foot shall slide.*[7]

And perhaps every soldier during the First World War knew this little prayer by heart:

> *Stay with me, God. The night is dark,*
> *The night is cold: my little spark*
> *Of courage dies. The night is long;*
> *Be with me, God, and make me strong.*[8]

The church, watching her best young men and women go out to defend freedom, has sung "Great Is Thy Faithfulness," a hymn based on the truth of this very passage: "Follow my decrees, . . . I . . . will not abandon my people Israel" (NIV). Jeremiah wrote it this way: "Because of the LORD'S great love we are not consumed, / for his compassions never fail. / They are new every morning; / great is your faithfulness" (Lam. 3:22–23 NIV).

Prayer: *God, root our natural pride in thankfulness. Except for our own civil struggles, never since the Revolution have we Americans felt the foot of the foreign oppressor. Help us to honor Your decrees as we use our ardor to defend Your causes throughout Your world.* ★

Lord, through this hour,

be thou our guide,

So by thy power no foot

shall slide.

A Good House

Unless the LORD builds the house,
They labor in vain who build it;
Unless the LORD guards the city,
The watchman stays awake in vain.

PSALM 127:1

A nation is like a large family. In such a family the inhabitants often quarrel and state their differences. But let anyone else attack that family, and all Americans as one will be swift to reply.

If we are a family, we are a romantic family. Brooks Atkinson wrote of our cheerful demeanor: "We Americans cheerfully assume that in some mystic way love conquers all, that good outweighs evil in the just balances of the universe, and that at the eleventh hour something gloriously triumphant will prevent the worst before it happens."[9]

Americans are sometimes fiercely romantic. It has been said that there is nothing wrong with Americans except their ideals. Yes, to this accusation—but we are a good family, often quarreling with each other but living together and defending each other. Why? Because our national philosophy is rooted in godly thinking. Americans seem to believe that God meant for the world to be an Eden of grace—a utopia, complete for the fellowship of God and all who took up His love.

In 1931 my father built a three-room house for his family of five.

This family of five would expand in the next decade to a family of nine. While the family grew larger, the house did not. But inside its very close walls its residents were crowded into a new kind of tolerance. Eleven people in a very small house have no secrets. Further, even our little petulances were understood to be trifles if any of us was threatened by someone outside our house. Then all nine of us quickly rallied around the endangered sibling. We were always ready to fight for the brother or sister under threat.

This perhaps is the greatest meaning of the phrase "proud house."

So it has been in the American family. We have had our family quarrels. Sometimes the Irish and English didn't get along as well as they might have. Cowboys and Indians had a few things to work out, as did the farmers and ranchers. But one or two bombs at Pearl Harbor, and we were all one with a big job to do. Whatever quarrels had occupied us, we suddenly stopped them, raised the flag, flew the grand eagle, and marched our patriotic way to victory.

America is a proud house.
Americans are a proud family!

Can we help but agree with the psalmist? "Unless the LORD builds the house, / They labor in vain who build it."

So we build.

So we are one family, insanely romantic, sometimes overly idealistic. But we are in love with a God who has the power to make our romance the ramparts of His kingdom and our idealism the bedrock reality of hope.

P r a y e r : *Lord, when prejudice raises its head, help us to remember we are a family. When we pass the homeless in the streets, help us to be openhanded and call needy souls our brethren. When any American is oppressed, help us to remember that they are part of us and we must labor together to build a perfect house, whose architect is higher than us, and whose dwelling more eternal.* ★

Day 6 | With wings like Eagles

The Purple Mountain Majesties

The heavens declare the glory of God;
And the firmament shows His handiwork.

Psalm 19:1

Stand in the maw of some great canyon and look up.
There you will see the God of anthems and the Creator of the blue canopy of space. In such a place you cannot doubt that the world has been born of a genius who always moves about the studio of His universe to color His canvas with glory.

The majesty that is America has caused her poets to praise the nation where craggy glaciers and snowy upthrusts seem to say, "Who never to himself has said, 'This is my native land'?"

That same majesty caused the psalmist to cry beneath the thrall of wide plains and rising peaks, "The earth is the LORD'S and all its fullness thereof." (Psalm 21:1). The proud grandeur that inspires Scriptures fills the breasts of patriots.

But mountains not only point to God, they seem to be the unbreakable backbone of the country. In the same way they have a way of appearing to be the Natural Altar, whose exalted tops are the last possible place where believers may reach out their hands toward the face of God.

What world religions have not had their specific mountain? The Greeks had Olympus. The Shinto faithful cast a worshipful eye on Fuji. The Hebrews received the law on Sinai. And while it is not a snowcapped peak, Christians adore the notion of Mt. Calvary or Mt. Olivet or the Mount of Ascension. Why all this fuss over mountains? Mountains point to God. They are natural places for high altars. Atop a mountain, away from the smoke and noise of the city, God can be felt. There, where the air is clean and cold, the lowland-loving crowds are missing. There God can talk to His world. There he can *get a word in edgewise* on how things ought to be.

If America has a mountain of altar grandeur, it must be Pikes Peak. It is far from America's highest mountain, but it stands strategically on the east wall of the Rockies, shouting to every dawdling wagon train: "Pass me with courage if you dare. Look at my summit, you who dream westward, and ask yourself, 'Am I able?' But remember this: the God, who sculpts the mountains, at first demands courage and later praise from all who pass my summit. If you would seek your fortunes in the broad valleys beyond me, then worship the God who crowns my craggy head with white. For this God is the true Glory. He is the maker of destiny and nations."

But the psalmist says that mountains do more than bear a silent witness to God's majesty. "Day unto day utters speech, And night unto night they reveal knowledge."

The mountains talk.

They praise.

They sing in the snow-driven winds that blast their frozen summits.

They laugh with holy laughter in a thousand cascades of frothy water.

They dance in sunlit rivers washing down to the sea.

And in every song they sing, "America is a God-crowned land."

In every breeze they whisper, "Surely such majesty is born in the heart of God, and speaks of His pure, unbroken love to a great land."

P r a y e r : *Lord, I lift up mine eyes to the hills and there You are. I lift up my heart in praise and there You are. I call out in my need and there You are— in love with me, in love with America. May both of us live to please You.* ✵

Lift Up your Heads, O You Gates

Lift up your heads, O you gates!
And be lifted up, you everlasting doors!
And the King of glory shall come in.

PSALMS 24:7

Second Samuel contains the wonderful account of King David bringing the Ark into the city of Jerusalem for the first time. Most believe that the Twenty-fourth Psalm was written to celebrate this event. Israel believed God Himself ruled the nation from His seat that was the *Kapporeth*—the lid of this box known as the Ark of the Covenant. So when the Ark entered Jerusalem it was a symbol to Israel that God Himself was coming into the city. Israel knew that no country could ever be free where God was excluded from dwelling in the capital.

See the grandeur of God's entrance to the palaces of power: the Ark passes up the high causeway, the gates of the city swing open, and the Ark comes into the city. Perhaps this very psalm was sung by all as the Ark entered Jerusalem:

Lift up your head, O you gates!
And the King of glory shall come in.

Envision such a scene in Washington, D.C. Imagine all people of faith

lining Pennsylvania Avenue with wild crowds exultantly singing:

> *Enter our nation, O God.*
> *Teach us your ways.*
> *Cause America to hunger after decency and morality.*
> *Cleanse our courts with justice,*
> *Fill our congress with totally honest men and women.*
> *Give us an anthem of togetherness:*
> *Instill in us a common pride,*
> *Sear across our eyes a complete vision of a nation that inspires*
> *justice worldwide.*

Then shall all Americans glory in the greatness. Then shall every patriot sing:

> *Lift up your head, O you gates,*
> *And the King of glory come in.*
> *Who is this King of glory?*
> *The God of America.*
> *The God of the Bible.*

The God who is the Father of our Lord Jesus Christ.
This God is the God of liberty.
He keeps the gates of freedom.
He invigorates our land with pride.

De Tocqueville said that America was like a temple. Our founding fathers understood our need to have God in the very center of government.

Upon my arrival in the United States, the religious aspect of the country was the first thing that struck my attention; and the longer I stayed there, the more did I perceive the great political consequences resulting from this state of things, to which I was accustomed. In France I had almost always seen the spirit of religion and the spirit of freedom pursuing courses diametrically opposed to each other; but in America I found they were intimately united, and that they reigned in common over the same country.[10]

How God and government should relate has always been and ever shall be debated. But the best of nations will never cease to care about how the Almighty regards behavior. The best will seek to serve God, that God who inspires their concern for the dispossessed peoples of the world.

P r a y e r : *God, may our cities be shrines of life. May our gates be the guardians of peace. May we lift up our heads in praise. May our gates swing open on hinges of compassion.* ★

As the Deer Thirsts After Water Brooks

As the deer pants for the water brooks,
So pants my soul for You, O God.
My soul thirsts for God, for the living God.
When shall I come and appear before God?

Psalm 42:1—2

There is a real sense in which the thirst for freedom is as real as the thirst for water. "Give me liberty or give me death," was Patrick Henry's great yearning from the soul. The psalmist knew a mysterious and more insurgent yearning—he yearned after God, and he likened his longing to that of a great stag made thirsty by his flight from the hunter. The animal's flight strains and tests every muscle of his body. He leaps from thicket to thicket and from crag to crag, all in his magnificent struggle to remain alive and free.

Freedom often requires such effort. To be free was the struggle of Ethan Allen with his patriot guerillas, who risked their lives in New England's woodlands. George Washington wintered at Valley Forge, testing his Colonial Army against the rigors of winter for the sake of freedom. John Hancock signed his name with oversized script on the Declaration of Independence so that all would see and never mistake his commitment to freedom.

What is it that marks the hunger and the thirst? It is an insatiable longing that drives the fleet stag to flight. But when the flight is over—when the danger has passed—liberty is its own reward. The prize ripples like cooling drafts of refreshment in streams of clear joy.

Steven Vincent Benet wrote so poignantly of this divine quest for freedom. He wrote a beautiful tale of one man's quest for freedom, that of a runaway slave named Cue whose perils were many. After one failed attempt to escape he was apprehended and returned to his owner who flogged him and put him into chains. Still the hunger to be free persisted, and so once again he made a run for that famous underground railroad that ended in Canada. When he awoke in Canada, he exulted in the fresh air of freedom.

Perhaps the great question is: Is the thirst for God and the thirst for liberty born of a common need? How closely they parallel each other. When Israel was in Egypt, she cried out for liberty. God heard her, and the Pharoah, under the heavy hand of God, at last set Israel free.

And Moses' great message of freedom was given to Israel on the way out of Egypt to the shining new land of Canaan, but in time—3,400 years of time—the message was inscribed on the Liberty Bell:

"Proclaim liberty throughout all the land". (Lev. 25:10)

In the wilderness God provided water from the rock. And Israel's thirst for water was slaked as she journeyed to that place where her thirst for national liberty would be abundantly supplied by God.

This same God shall give water to the thirsty deer and freedom to those who thirst for it and are to pay for it with the price of discipline.

> Prayer: *Lord, I thirst to know Your love. I yearn to live in this good land. So fill my desire for love by causing me to trust in You. Then slake my thirst for liberty by making me a responsible American.* ★

THEY SHALL MOUNT UP
WITH WINGS

But those who wait on the LORD
Shall renew their strength;
They shall mount up with wings like eagles,
They shall run and not be weary,
They shall walk and not faint.

ISAIAH 40:31

The eagle, since colonial times, has been the American symbol that appears on American money, banners, and presidential seals.
Eagles also are mentioned in Scripture. In Isaiah 40:31, the eagle is the
soaring image of those whose stamina and discipline causes them to
soar in life. Isaiah used eagles to symbolize the inner status of the
heart, where God lives in us and is enduring. But God does not merely wake us to the wonder of Himself, He wakes us to an understand-
ing of that good passion that makes us surrender our plodding ways,
to see them transferred to wings. Once we have learned the art of soaring as eagles with God, we marvel that we were ever content to travel
any other way.

God is the source of all soaring. Dwight David Eisenhower said
in his inaugural address on January 20, 1953, "Whatever America
brings to pass in the world, must first come to pass in the heart of

America."[11] Nations do not trust God and soar by the common will. If nations soar it is only because their individual citizens have learned to do it.

The most eagles I ever saw gathered in one place was in the city landfill outside Ketchiken, Alaska. They appeared to be gathered there to feed on garbage. It was not an easy image for me to absorb, and I confess it is not a symbol I have much pleasure in remembering. If I could I would blot from my mind these grand American icons that were so occupied with scavenging they had no time for soaring.

The image haunts me.

I remember what an American judge said in a court trial of 1844: "The morality of the country is deeply engrafted upon Christianity . . . We are a people whose manners are refined and whose morals have been elevated and inspired with a more enlarged benevolence by means of the Christian religion."[12]

Eagles in garbage dumps hold a kind of reprimand to all Americans. The question the image begs is not, "What should the country do to be a more moral place for me to live?" The real issue is, "What kind of person do I need to be to make the country a place where eagles soar?"

There is always the tendency to cry, "In whose heart must any moral principle find its life? Is it not in the heart of others—of someone else? Is there not some more patriotic person who could pay the price of liberty?" No. Liberty must be the practice of every heart, starting with ourselves. Unless the banner waves inside us, there is little use setting it on a staff.

When each one cherishes faith and every individual trusts in the Lord, then idealistic patriotism and spiritual power may soar with the eagles.

P r a y e r : *Lord let me trust You that I may soar. Teach me to depend upon You and to be the better person that You created me to be—teach me to soar. For then the wings of liberty will have come.* ✭

HE WHO TILLS THE LAND WILL HAVE PLENTY OF BREAD

I have been young, and now am old;
Yet I have not seen the righteous forsaken,
Nor his descendants begging bread.

PSALM 37:25

"I am old and have been young," is the testimony of
the psalmist, "yet abundance is still the best definition of God."
God's gifts are a cornucopia of grain and oil and wine, tilted
downward and spilling out over America. God's goodness is
flowing over the Napa Valley and the golden plains of Kansas.
God's goodness is in the scarlet kisses in the orchards of
Washington and the pecan plantations of Georgia. God's smile
ripens the groves of Orlando in brilliant, flame-colored fruit.

"America! America! God shed His grace on thee," we sing.

There are some who say this pledge of abundance is too
simple. "He who owns this land will have plenty of bread,"
some say is a false proverb. What of the homeless? What of
the starving masses of the world? What of those whose long-
ago hard times still cause them to complain of life in the
"dirty thirties"?

In the fifties I worked in the wheat harvest between Kingfisher, Oklahoma, and Mandan, North Dakota. It is perhaps a fault in all of us that we do not treasure the best parts of our lives as we live through them. But now, with maturity and perspective, I can see that they were better years than I thought them to be. I was baptized in summer gold. The grain rippled first on the reels of combines, which slashed at the liquid fields. Then through the gentle hammering of the machine, grain gushed as molten metal into the bin of our huge machines.

I bent my back in moving that grain with a scoop as it ladled the splendor from the auger-spout to the wheat truck. Now I could see the glory of God. It wasn't just that we were cutting wheat and hauling it harvested from the field, but we were providing bread for our nation and those distant nations where bread was scarce.

We were helping God with His all-consuming business of abundance. Abundance is not what happens when the rain is good and the sun is faithful. Abundance is the attitude of God. The word is not a synonym for "too much." It is a synonym for

the ever-ample providence of America's Lover.

But there is an obligation in being loved. The obligation says that our bread was not given to us to spoil us with indulgence. God's bread is a covenant of substance in which the Giver gives so that the receiver may return worship. Beyond the harvest the grateful can offer the blessing to others whose fortune is less and whose very existence demands that those who have so lavishly received learn lavish giving.

Even a thin harvest in a lean decade should cause us to remember that all gifts come from God. It should remind us that to hoard God's blessings is to lose them. It is rarely those who are filled with abundance who see God's abundance. Those who surfeit in wealth take all of God's supplies as though they had furnished their own bread. It is the once hungry who see the cornucopia and exalt their little loaves toward heaven. These adore the God whose abundance comes sometimes in little bits to be magnified by praise.

America is well-schooled in the blessed art of national thanksgiving. The national eye has been made clear by true sight. We are certain of the psalmist's declaration,

I am old and have been young,
But I have never seen the righteous forsaken,
Nor his seed begging bread.

P r a y e r : *Lord, thank You for this good land. Thank You for the faithful promise of seedtime and harvest. Thank you for the rain and the grain and the loaf. Thank You for America, whose abundance in its season feeds the world. And most of all, thank You for my daily bread.* ★

"I am old and have been young,"

A Light to the Nations

Arise, shine;
For your light has come!
And the glory of the LORD is risen upon you.
For behold, the darkness shall cover the earth,
And deep darkness the people;
But the LORD will arise over you,
And His glory will be seen upon you.
The Gentiles shall come to your light,
And kings to the brightness of your rising.

Isaiah 60:1–3

That great sculpture that we call the Statue of Liberty was called by its sculptor, Bartholdi, *Liberty Enlightening the World.* It is perhaps the greatest symbol of freedom in the world. How often the word *free* occurs in the Bible! Consider this catalogue of but a few:

- Psalms 146:7: "The LORD gives the freedom to the prisoners."
- John 8:32: "You shall know the truth, and the truth shall make you free."
- Romans 6:18: "You have been set free from sin." (NIV)
- Revelation 1:5: "[Christ] washed us from our sins in His own blood."
- 2 Corinthians 3:17: "Where the Spirit of the Lord is, there is liberty."

God must care about liberty for He said to Moses in the wilderness, "I have heard the cry of those in bondage in Egypt. I have heard the cry of my people, Israel." It was perhaps the horror of slavery that awakened our country to the need for the Civil War. And if it can be said that there are important wars of conscience, surely the Civil War was one. America still has not totally resolved all ethnic oppression, but she has settled her definitions of right and wrong on the issue. It was more than a hundred years after the American Civil War settled the question of slavery that Americans put pressure on South Africa to take the pressure from her bloody civil struggles and greet all people as free.

Americans feel very strongly that her hard-won lessons on the subject of freedom are not to be hoarded. The moment we say that this freedom is only for us, we are saying that slavery is all right as long as we're not the slaves. It is an odd doctrine indeed that teaches that freedom has no obligation except to enjoy itself. Of course, it has an obligation. Its obligation is to look around and see those who are still shackled. It must not see without pitying those who are yet in chains.

Liberty comes as light. It makes obvious the dark, invisible

sufferings of those who are chained. It is bold enough to stand before an armored tank in Tiananmen Square. It topples the statues of tyrants in St. Petersburg. It breaks down walls in Germany. It marches in rags through India. It cries from the lips of Scottish Highlanders. It strengthens Tibetans in the rugged passages of their exile.

While light makes no noise, it cannot be silenced. It leaks through the fissures between the fingers of our hands. It spills over the rims of canyons and slides in moonlit silver down canyon pinnacles. It flies in space from newborn stars and hides as sparkles in the eyes of visionaries.

So Bartholdi was right. Liberty flies against darkness. It does indeed "enlighten the world." Emma Lazarus was right:

> *Here at our sea-washed, sunset gates shall stand*
> *a mighty woman with a torch. Whose name*
> *is Mother of Exiles. From her beacon hand*
> *glows worldwide welcome.*

And if Isaiah were to have written the poem it might read:

You are under obligation America.
Arise and shine for your light has come . . .
Nations will come to your light
And Kings to the brightness of your dawn.

P r a y e r : *Lord, we who have the light must remember that America is in the export business, and that our greatest export is freedom. Help us never to forget that America's chief business is spiritual light and power. Help us to see that the only way light may be preserved at home is to make sure it is scattered freely among the nations.* ★

Here at our sea-washed, sunset gates

shall stands a mighty woman

with a torch . . . and her name is

Mother of Exiles. From her beacon

hand glows worldwide welcome.

Righteousness and Community

Righteousness exalts a nation,
But sin is a reproach to any people.

When God examines our hearts, righteousness is a response of respect. God is our Father, and what good parents have not craved from their children good behavior? But nations never arrive at morality by group consensus. They never become more moral than the individual citizens who compose them. How does a person or a nation arrive at that place where it loses the connection between the pleasure it brings to God and its moral permissiveness?

The grand sins that steal a nation's godliness begin with those citizens who tell themselves that how they behave is their own business. How odd that a man unfaithful to his marriage vows rarely sees himself as a contributor to national immorality. A woman who forgets to honor her motherly responsibility may not see her neglect as sin and rarely sees herself as a significant player in the national decline of morality.

National immorality is but the sum of its citizens' permissiveness. The problem is that Main Street appears unchanged by the sins

of it citizens. The flags still fly! The band still marches! But the sins of every citizen war against all that may be called true community. For the unseen flaws in the human spirit work tiny fissures in the solidarity of our national foundations. And when the morality of the heart is flawed enough, the columns crumble in the forum.

The Romans gave the world the miracle of concrete. They built as the Greeks never had. Their roads and aqueducts and temples grew until the Mediterranean was a solid testament to firm, unyielding architecture. But slowly, ever so slowly, the empire of firm concrete was eaten away by what the Romans believed were their own private lives. Only too late did Rome discover that immorality is never private and empires of concrete are at last destroyed by the collective permissions of undisciplined hearts. Immorality and indecency are at first attractive to the foolish. Then they become an habitual way of living. Finally they are addictions who swallow people and nations. Perhaps many Romans never saw the connection between their own behavior and what was happening in the nation as a whole.

This denial is a recognized symptom of addiction. A drunkard rises and drinks each day thinking, insanely, that *somehow today things will turn out differently—better.* He clearly believes that his life will arrive

at moral perfection, or at least progress, without any personal obligation. Only a fierce desire for righteousness can exalt this man. We must hold ourselves accountable, and God is waiting.

"What's wrong with America?" asked one of her patriots. Then he sadly concluded, "I am . . . I'm what's wrong with America." America will endure only so long as the flag over the courthouse is no more important than the secret banners of the heart.

> P r a y e r : *Lord, it is Your command that I live in obedience, disciplining my temptations and ordering my life after Your expectations. Help me never to forget that it matters how I live—that I cannot expect the nation I love to be any more moral at its heart than I have been in mine.* ★

How Lovely Is Your Tabernacle

How lovely is Your tabernacle,
O LORD of hosts!

Psalm 84:1

Alexis de Tocqueville said that America was a great nation with the soul of a church. Bernard Baruch said, "The highest and best form of efficiency is the spontaneous cooperation of a free people." So here is Christ's greatest gift to humankind—the church! Here is where America keeps her soul and where free people are at their best. Here in churches—often very small churches—Americans pray for the courage to serve liberty whatever the cost. Here, in great cathedrals or rural chapels, little plaques adorn the walls, reciting the names of those whose blood was spilled to keep the nation free.

When I was a pastor, I officiated at many funerals for American Veterans. In contrast to the funerals I did for the many civilians across the years, these "military" funerals always affected me. It was a good affectation—perhaps, even a noble affectation. It said that in this moment we weren't just burying a brother, we were acknowledging that he had lived and died a little differently from the rest of us. He had once gone somewhere in the world to make the world safe for democracy.

So I always got an odd grip in the pit of my stomach when I faced a flag-draped coffin. The haunting echo of twenty-one rounds of rim-fire reminded me that this person had faced artillery and gunfire to serve the very flag that now swaddled him in death. Now at last he settled into the good earth of his homeland.

Twenty-one guns!

A folded banner!

The distant wail of taps from the golden bell of a bugle held in a white-gloved hand!

Americans know the price of liberty and have never considered it too dear to pay.

Americans have never gotten over their need to make the church their "sending-out" place for those consecrated soldiers who somehow saw their own cause as God's.

There are many who cry, "Never paint Christ in red, white, and blue! Jesus wore a robe and not a flag!" But many a soldier has left his homeland breathing Psalm 84:1–4, "How lovely is Your tabernacle . . . Blessed are those who dwell in Your house; / They will still be praising You." And there in the church Americans still find their soul in simple rites of confirmation or communion. Baptism and

confession are how Americans declare, "We are His people and the sheep of His pasture. / Enter into His gates with thanksgiving, / and into His courts with praise" (Ps. 100:3–4).

Here in the little country chapels is born a longing that lives in yearning from battlefields—the strong yearning to return home. Perhaps that is why Woodrow Wilson remarked in asking Congress for a declaration of war, "America is privileged to spend her blood and her might for the principles that gave her birth and happiness and peace which she has treasured. God helping her she can do no other."[13] But home for God-fearing Americans in war or peace is always the house of God.

Hoist a steeple, sing an anthem: there you will find the heart of America.

P r a y e r : *Lord, here I give You that cache of reminiscences most treasured: my childhood church—the school of all my values, the ground of all my virtues, and the inward portrait of my own love for You. Bless every pastor who understands that sermons are the bread of integrity, hymns are the music of morality, and prayers are the linking of Your supply with our own fragile existence.* ✶

Let Everyone Who Thirsts Come to the Waters

The new colossus
Not like to brazen giant of Greek fame,
with conquering limbs astride from land to land;
Here at your sea-washed, sunset gates shall stand
a mighty woman with a torch
whose flame is imprisoned lightning,
and her name is Mother of Exiles.
From her beacon-hand glows
world-wide welcome;
her mild eyes command the air bridged harbor
that twin cities frame.
"Keep ancient lands your storied pomp!"
cries she with silent lips.
"Give me your tired, your poor,
your huddled masses of your teeming shore.
Send these, the homeless, tempest tost to me.
I lift my lamp beside the golden door!"

Emma Lazarus (1849–1887)

The nineteenth-century invitation to come to America drew immigrants with the attraction of a lodestone. Impoverished men and women crossed the sea at the lure of freedom. Some were drawn by the hope for land. Some came longing for a second chance. The call to America came framed in optimism. Lyndon Johnson said in his State of the Union Message on January 17, 1968, "Our ship is moving through troubled new waters, toward new and better shores."[14]

That sense of hope, that undying futurism called the world to Ellis Island and flexed its optimism on the grand desire to start again. John F. Kennedy said in 1960, "The American by nature is optimistic. He is experimental, an inventor and a builder who builds best when called upon to build greatly."[15] This undying optimism is rooted in the soil of the immigrant's hope. He landed on Ellis Island, boasting, "I'm here, America! Give me any square foot of your grace, and I will forever call Columbia the place of my rebirth. America! Land of God and the second chance!"

Isaiah presaged the anthem of American hope and optimism in his call to the exiles. He called the weary to come to the waters of Zion to wash and revitalize their dull, despair-crusted spirits:

Come, all you who are thirsty, come to the waters;
and you who have no money, come, buy and eat!
Come, buy wine and milk without money and without cost . . .
Surely you will summon nations you know not,
and nations that do not know you will hasten to you.
(Isa. 55:1, 5 NIV).

And so Isaiah's exiles came. They drank of the deep, cool waters of personal freedom, but they did not do so selfishly. When their thirst was slaked, they bottled the vintage of human freedom and exported their liberty worldwide.

Freedom! One of the best things in life. The best things in life are free, but they are never cheap and seldom easy. In some ways civil freedom is like salvation itself. Redemption was bought by Jesus and paid for with His very life. It is the whole point of grace that God gave us this life free and clear—no strings attached! Gifts are like that. They are always free, but only to the receiver. They often cost the giver everything.

One Christian convert, shortly after coming to faith in Christ, was told by his pastor that he might want to consider giving an

offering each week to the church. "After all," said the pastor, "the church does a great deal of good in the world community. It ministers to the sick and dispenses the gospel around the world. Every Christian must give to establish the kingdom in the world."

"But," protested the new Christian, "I thought the water of life was free."

"It is indeed," said the pastor, "but someone has to pay for the waterworks!"

The water of American liberty is free to all Americans, but all of us who drink of that water must pay for the waterworks. Each time congress adopts a new budget, we are all asked to pay to secure our liberty. The cost is little; the water, most refreshing.

> Prayer: *Lord, You have established a nation whose greatest expanses were not given to build skyscrapers or sprawling ranches. The greatest of those expanses was the room to build dreams; and the dreams, when hatched, produced a race of people giant in generosity. Thank You for making me an American. Now make me responsible for being the best American I can be with an oversized longing for character and morality.* ★

Come, all you who are thirsty,

come to the waters;

and you who have no money, come,

buy and eat!

Isa. 55:1 NIV

THE LOVE OF GOD FOR A GODLY NATION

When Israel was a child, I loved him,
And out of Egypt I called My son.
As they called them,
So they went from them;
They sacrificed to the Baals,
And burned incense to carved images.

I taught Ephraim to walk,
Taking them by their arms;
But they did not know that I healed them.
I drew them with gentle cords,
With bands of love,
And I was to them as those who
take the yoke from their neck.
I stooped and fed them.

HOSEA 11:1–4

Hosea, the Old Testament prophet, reminded the people of Israel that the reason for their greatness as a nation was that God very much loved them: "When Israel was a child, I loved him, / . . . I taught Ephraim to walk, / Taking them by their arms; / . . . I healed them. / . . . I was to them as those who take the yoke from their neck. / I stooped and fed them." In this tender passage God's love for Israel is rehearsed. But there is something flawed in the love they returned to God. They became self-willed. They ignored their godly heritage, and God had to deal firmly with them.

Will Rogers said, "If we ever pass out as a great nation we ought to put on our tombstone, 'America died from the delusion that she had moral leadership.'"[16]

Moral leadership! This was the explicit goal of the Puritans who, having landed on Plymouth Rock, determined to be a moral colony in the new world and export those Bible-based values to the world. John Winthrop reminded those newly arrived Puritans of the consequences of forgetting those goals:

> *We are a company professing ourselves fellow-members of Christ . . . knit together by this bond of love . . . We are entered into covenant with Him for*

his work . . . For we must consider that we shall be as a city set on a hill, the eyes of all people are upon us; so that if we deal falsely with our God in this work we have undertaken and so cause Him to withdraw His present help from us, we shall be made a story and a byword throughout the world.[17]

Is there a guarantee that our land will not diminish in its holiest intentions? One thing is sure, our wholeness can never move confidently into the future if we lose our way in multicultural struggles. We are one people, and no ethnic or previous national allegiances should be allowed to erase our oneness. Then we will have fulfilled the image of God's universal fatherhood on this great, diverse, but never-to-be-divided nation.

To be American is to commit ourselves to protect and guarantee our future. Henry Cabot Lodge gave us this most important instruction:

Let every man honor and love the land of his birth and the race from which he springs and keep the memory green. It is a pious and honorable duty. But let us have done with British Americans and Irish Americans and

German Americans and so on, and all be Americans . . . If a man is going to be an American at all let it be so without any qualifying adjectives.[18]

P r a y e r : *God, there can be little doubt that You are a God of love. It comes to us in such simple things as daybreak or a spring rain. But it comes in more forceful ways in the beauty of our national heritage. We have received so much, and we stand at the feet of so many heroes; we cannot doubt we are loved. We praise You for touching us with grace and creating our nation as a forum for liberty.* ★

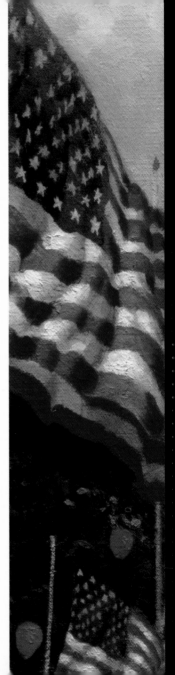

Let every man honor and love

the land of his birth and

the race from which he springs and

keep the memory green.

THE ART OF GOING HOME

"Now, therefore," says the LORD,
"Turn to Me with all your heart,
With fasting, with weeping, and with mourning."
So rend your heart, and not your garments;
Return to the LORD your God,
For He is gracious and merciful,
Slow to anger, and of great kindness;
And He relents from doing harm.

JOEL 2:12–13

God has placed a homing instinct in all of our hearts. He is eager that we worship Him and that our love for Him never ceases. But whose walk is so constant that it has not sometimes wandered away from God? So there exists a call from God that we—who have wandered away from love—come back, that we return home to Him.

In *The Rise and Fall of the Third Reich*, the little town of Lidice, Czechoslovakia, was singled out by the Führer to cite as an example of terror. A German overlord had been assassinated there, and since none—if they knew the assassin—was willing to reveal the name, the S.S. decided to punish the whole town. On one horrible day of terror, all the males more than twelve years of age were lined up on one side

of a double column and executed before their terrified women. Their wives and children in the other line were loaded into cattle cars and taken to concentration camps far from their tiny village where they either died or lived through the horrors of the camp until their release in 1945.

Finally, after all had been killed or exiled, a bulldozer came into the little city and leveled the town. Then the debris from houses and businesses were burned. Then tractors and plows came in and plowed up the ground where the village had been, and finally the former village site was sowed with grass seed to match the grassy hills of the surrounding area. There was nothing left of Lidice to say it had ever existed.

One of the women who survived concentration camp said that while the execution of her husband and her own deportment had been inexpressible horror, she was not prepared for the shock of coming over the brow of the hill before Lidice. The sheer horror of seeing nothing wounded her at even deeper levels than the earlier Nazi horrors.

Going home! This must be the most powerful of all yearnings.

All that may be said of individuals may be said of nations. God

considered Israel His very special child. When she had wandered away from Him He desired that she come back to Him. It was the custom of ancient Israelites, when they found themselves in grief, to tear their garments as a symbol of their sorrow. God wants arrogant self-sufficiency to yield to Him in new humility. He is even now calling America to turn from her waywardness and return to Him.

P r a y e r : *Lord, nothing so convinces us of America's value as travel abroad. American tourists want to see the world. But when they do the words* home *and* America *become synonyms. God, we thank You for this great land, set between oceans and crowned with peace. We thank You that it is our home.* ✦

THE REFRESHING OF GOD

And it shall come to pass afterward
That I will pour out My Spirit on all flesh;
Your sons and your daughters shall prophesy,
Your old men shall dream dreams,
Your young men shall see visions.

JOEL 2:28

God is great! All the Bible establishes that! But in passages like this, the Bible speaks of the life-changing nearness of God. It is not enough that God be lofty and powerful; there are those moments when all of us want God near. When God comes near, wonderful things begin to happen. A dull people become visionary. The timid are given new courage. Old men, who felt that life had passed them by, suddenly feel that God is making them useful once again.

This is the marvelous work of God, and His agency is Himself—the Holy Spirit. He comes washing the world with newness, cleansing old hurt and promising the helpless that heaven has heard their cry and acted in behalf of their need. All of these things occur when God visits His people.

But perhaps the greatest gift of all is vision. When we feel the force of some new dream welling up within us, we are most alive. It

was Columbus who wrote most beautifully of the power of the Holy Spirit to endue His people with vision. Concerning his famous voyage, he wrote in his log book,

> *Our Lord opened my understanding (I could sense His hand upon me) so it became clear to me that the voyage was feasible . . . All those who heard about my enterprise rejected it with laughter, scoffing at me . . . Who doubts that this illumination was from the Holy Spirit? I attest that the Spirit with marvelous rays of light, consoled me through the holy and sacred Scriptures . . . they inflame me with a sense of great urgency . . . No one should be afraid to take on any enterprise in the name of our Savior if it is right and if the purpose is purely for His holy service . . . And I say that the sign which convinces me that our Lord is hastening in the end of the world is the preaching of the Gospel recently in so many lands.*[19]

The Holy Spirit is indeed the giver of the most selfless visions. None of us have discovered anything so dramatic as did Christopher Columbus, but who of us have not here and there awakened to some great dream of which only God can be the Author? But then that's the great value of America. Not every American vision has come from the

Holy Spirit, but all of them came from inspired souls who felt they had enough room here to invent, create, and change their world. So in America the industrial revolution found room to grow and to export all it expressed.

But America's best export may be vision itself. If even little people have room to imagine, the world is better for it. And lately it seems across the Pacific, people in a score of Asian countries are learning the valuable lessons of incentive and imagination. The entire Pacific Rim is coming alive with individual vision, and the force of Asian creativity is as powerful as can be imagined. Still, in surveying the power of the Asian Renaissance, who can help but wonder where they got the idea.

P r a y e r :   *Lord, send Your Spirit, as You once did on the day of Pentecost. Awake Americans to new levels of bold ideas. Give visionaries greater vision. Resurrect dead minds with new dreams. Then perhaps the dove will descend and all peoples of the earth will wake to the splendor.* ★

Seek Good and Not Evil, That You May Live

Seek good and not evil,
That you may live;
So the LORD God of hosts will
be with you,
As you have spoken.
Hate evil, love good;
Establish justice in the gate.
It may be that the LORD God of hosts
Will be gracious to the
remnant of Joseph.

Amos 5:14–15

America has a most simple creed: "Be good!"

Who can keep it for all its simplicity?

But the simplicity of the creed suggests that life is a matter of continual moral choices. Amos adds to this issue of moral choice the notion that those who choose good live, and those who choose evil die. Those who choose good reap character. Daniel Webster has written of Washington what I think must be true of all people who consistently make good moral choices:

America has furnished to the world the character of Washington, and if our American institutions had done nothing else, that alone would have entitled them to the respect of mankind.[20]

When moral people possess a nation, they live, and the quality of their lives furnishes the world with life.

Seeking good seems an old and out-of-date quest these days. The entertainment industry has no patience for humble men seeking peace. The big money comes out for revenge and libertine lusts. Why? Who can say, in a world where children tote guns to school and terrorists explode bombs in office buildings. It would seem that we would do well to return to a world that seeks good.

There is but a single letter of difference between the word *God* and the word *good*. They are essentially the same word. The lofty Bible word for "good" is the word *righteousness*. And God's great call has always been one of asking people to concern themselves with righteousness. But how do we seek righteousness? There is only one way: seek God. God looks with favor on our lives when we behave ourselves. We please God when we learn to behave and teach the value of prizing good behavior to our children.

Seeking good, as Amos presents it, has the character of moral drivenness. In the best of people—and certainly in the best of national leaders—there is a hunger for good. In such a world nobody is looking for shortcuts, and nobody wants to bilk a neighbor. Good is a quality that says honor is preferred. Character grows not from doing right but from the hunger to do right.

Those who hunger to do good live long and prosperous lives. But nations that never forget the imperative of seeking good have stacked centuries on their side. They thrive and do well, and their goodness is never abandoned nor is God's protection and blessing in their lives.

> P r a y e r : *Lord make it clear that to do good is to survive. Make goodness my desire, and clothe our nation with the same passion for right.* ✱

THE RIGHTEOUS STREAM

But let justice run down like water,
And righteousness like a mighty stream.

AMOS 5:24

These famous words of the prophet Amos adorn the memorial of Martin Luther King, Jr. The statement is more than the epitaph of a great man, however. It would be even more suitable as the motto of a great nation. Perhaps Martin Luther King, Jr. more than any other man proved that justice can be achieved. He, of course, had a dream—that every American should enjoy the same kind of liberty in the same way as all others.

But Martin Luther King, Jr. realized how very hard justice was to come by. Sometimes—in fact, most times—many must challenge some decadent prejudice to see virtue born in its place. So it was with Martin Luther King, Jr. It must have seemed at times that he was losing. Perhaps when he sweltered in the Birmingham jail it must have seemed that proud Wrong would never be humble enough to confess her injustices. He might even have remembered those famous words of William Cullen Bryant:

Truth forever on the scaffold, wrong forever on the throne—
Yet that scaffold sways the future and beyond the dim unknown,
Standeth God within the shadows keeping watch above His own.

Justice must roll down like waters and righteousness as an ever-flowing stream.

It was this very theme of injustice that inspired America's war for independence. But having won that war long ago, are we still the champions of the world's dispossessed? Do we struggle to rise to the defense of those who have no strength left to defend themselves? Does every American own the right to have justice, whether or not they know where to get it and whether or not they can pay for it? Each of us must care.

Martin Luther King, Jr. was a preacher. In some ways he did not do a very complicated thing, only the right thing. He simply challenged people to do justly. The words *just* and *justice* are rooted in the same word and in a very real way stand opposite to the words they came to replace: *prejudge* or *prejudice*. To execute real judgment, said King, was to set aside your prejudgments.

How is that to be done? Well, he showed us how. It is as simple as

gathering around in circles and singing "We Shall Overcome." As Americans we once gathered in circles—white hands holding black hands—and we sang about overcoming. We learned a great lesson by singing in circles. We found out that when we cared enough to sing of triumph we already had done it.

When we find those who justly deserve retribution, may we remember that grace gave us more than we ever deserved. Having received mercy from our God, let us dispense mercy to the undeserving. In such a way justice is upgraded to Christlikeness.

Prayer: *Lord, make the world just, but make me merciful. Help me not to demand that others give me what I deserve, but help me to forgive my debtors even as I have been forgiven.* ✭

GOD'S REQUIREMENT
FOR AMERICA

He has shown you, O man, what is good;
And what does the LORD require of you
But to do justly,
To love mercy,
And to walk humbly with your God?

MICAH 6:8

Endurance and justice are bedfellows. Micah knew this and insisted that justice was the character of great nations. When world-builders are just, the worlds that they build will endure.

Steven Vincent Benet wrote:

Broad-streeted Richmond . . .
The trees in the streets are old trees used to living with people,
Family trees that remember your grandfather's name.[21]

The world will live and age like mighty oaks as long as it remembers that laws exist to make all the world safe for the rich and poor alike. But the moment the law goes on sale and the highest bidder owns the judges, the poor are sold for shoes and the rich soon swagger in the

smugness of hedonism.

It is a small wonder that the prophet Micah called the nation to justice. He knew the truths later spoken by William Pitt: "Unlimited power is apt to corrupt the minds of those who possess it; and this I know, my lords, that where the law ends, tyranny begins."[22] Therefore we are all called to care about law. We are all called to insist that the wealthy cannot buy it and the poor must not reckon with it falsely merely to get gain.

It was also William Pitt who reminded us that even if we abrogate the laws of God, or perjure our way through human tribunals, we still must reckon with God whose justice at last settles all wrong precisely with no appeals: "There is something behind the throne greater than the King himself."[23] And what is that? The Divine Last Word. The Eternal King of Everlasting Values.

The simple ideas of Micah have become the foundations of our republic: We must do justly, love mercy, and walk humbly with our God. Stop and consider these simple values that are foundational to America. What a heavy marble empire is built on simple truths. Does the capitol building seem large and stable to you? It is secure only as long as it clings to this simplicity, straight from the heart of this Old

Testament prophet. The endurance of marble empires is fragile when they forget their charter. Jesus once gestured to the mighty buildings of the temple and said, "Do you see all these things? I tell you there will not be one stone left upon another." Jesus reminded them that the greatest of buildings are only as stable as the endurance of the simple truths that undergird them. The moral foundations of America are not complicated, but the power in their simplicity has awakened the world to fair play and an awareness that if God isn't pleased with America's sense of mercy and justice, there is no national dream of consequence. Behind great nations lies this very simple truth: it is necessary to keep rehearsing the founding simplicity so the nation can endure.

Prayer: *Lord, help us to make a threefold rule of Micah's words: help us to act justly, so that we are never unlawful. Help us to love mercy, so that we are always kind. And, finally, help walk us to walk humbly with You, so that we do not manufacture some foolish arrogance that not only separates us from You but keeps us from being human in a needy time.* ★

TRUSTING GOD IN THE HARD TIMES

Though the fig tree may not blossom,
Nor fruit be on the vines;
Though the labor of the olive may fail,
And the fields yield no food;
Though the flock may be cut off from the fold,
And there be no herd in the stalls—
Yet I will rejoice in the LORD,
I will joy in the God of my salvation.

HABAKKUK 3:17–18

The Great Depression was the epitome of the hard times for many Americans. Habakkuk said hard times would come. There would be times, said the prophet, when the fig tree would not bud and there would be no grapes on the vines. During those times the fields would produce no food, and there would be no sheep in the pens or cattle in the stalls. But even during those times Habakkuk was exultant, "Yet I will rejoice in the LORD, / I will joy in the God of my salvation."

Why has America weathered the hard times so well? Because she has never withheld compassion against her countrymen when

her countrymen were in need. "Brother, can you spare a dime?" was the oft-asked question of the streets in the early thirties. Americans could spare dimes when pocket change counted. In Colossians 3:12 (NIV) the apostle Paul furnished the recipe for American togetherness in the hard times: "Clothe yourselves with compassion." It is God's advice to the merciful. It is grand counsel to all needy souls to selflessly combine their poverty together and see how abundance results.

The key to national compassion is not wealth. Compassion has never been a matter of those who are rich giving to the poor. The rich, with only a few exceptions, have never been so motivated. Compassion is usually a matter of poor people helping each other. It is also rather true that the wealthy often refuse to see God as the source of their wealth. The wealthy often visit the clubs, reading to each other from *How to Be the Self-Made Man*.

Not so with the poor. Never having tomorrow's or next week's rent secure, they are convinced that the sheer source of all they receive has come from God. It is the poor who thank God for their daily bread. It can be easy for a wealthy person to forget

these things, yet it is so inspiring when they do not.

But Habakkuk saw the hard times as the point at which God steps into our insufficiency with His greatness. He does, as the apostle suggested, supply our needs according to His riches in Glory. Therefore He is trustworthy. But God is never more trustworthy than when we remember that He is there regardless of status.

I have lived through several national crises: World War II, the Cuban Missile Crisis, the Kent State killings, and the Hundred Hour War. In all of these times, I saw God become real to millions of Americans. What shall we do? Lament that the crisis came so that we were forced to call on God? Of course not. The crises are a part of the call to prayer, the prayer is a forcing of our faces toward God, and God is the rewarder of all who will diligently seek Him. The crisis is the need that forges nations into oneness and causes derelicts to pick up the great things they laid by in the good times. Need makes us ask. Asking is the way we seek. Seeking causes us to knock at the door of God. And, of course, knocking always opens it.

P r a y e r : *Lord, when times are hard You are there, and when You are there, times don't seem so hard. Give me a spirit of thanksgiving, even if there is no turkey on the table. Help me bless Your abundance even when I cannot manage it on my own and have to trust others to afford me Your supply of daily bread. Help me to remember that if I can praise You when I have no bread, I will better remember to thank You during the times when all my needs are saturated in Your abundance.* ✵

Yet I will rejoice in

the LORD,

I will joy in the God

of my salvation.

HABAKKUK 3:18

God's Measurement of Democracy

Then I raised my eyes and looked,
and behold, a man with a measuring line in his hand.

Zechariah 2:1

In a stern vision, the prophet Zechariah saw a man with a measuring line in his hand. It was clear to him that God was about to measure the nation to see where her compassion was too short and her immorality was too long. Following the vision, Zechariah heralded this truth: righteousness blesses a nation, but immorality abases a nation. Virtue is the key to God's abundance; sin always meets judgment.

Zechariah's vision was an image of God as He measured the moral dimensions of empires. God then sent His servants to announce that the dimensions of national morality did not measure up.

In the book of Daniel is the story of a Babylonian king who, in the midst of a drunken orgy, saw the scrawling fingers of a man's hand write national judgement on the palace wall. The famous words were, *"Mene, Mene, Tekel, Upharsin."* Those words meant: "You have been weighed in the balances and found wanting. Your kingdom is taken from you and given to another."

Historian Arnold Toynbee pointed out that twenty-eight civilizations before our own have come and gone. They nearly all came in with intense patriotism and went out surfeiting in their own immorality. They were measured by God, found to be morally short, and replaced.

Surely there is not a sensitive American who does not cast up to heaven two prayers that come yoked like oxen in the fields of God. First of all, we cannot wake on any day without being thankful for the liberty that is ours. Second, we cannot have failed to notice that not far from the Statue of Liberty is Times Square, where pornography and other evil is easily accessible. And when we see these rampant destructive qualities so near the Lady of the Harbor, are we not prone to ask, "Is it not time to raise a new statue—the Statue of Responsibility?"

Perhaps we should raise this Statue of Responsibility in San Francisco, and then, when all Americans have learned to live halfway between the Statue of Liberty and the Statue of Responsibility, we will have become a people of great civic liberty and high moral responsibility.

God is ever at the door of every great nation. He always comes with a measuring line. God does not carry the line seeking to measure the culture so that He can obtain a picture of her moral size. He knows

all things and certainly knows the moral size of America. He is measuring the nation for her benefit. What God asks America is this: Does the country know where she is falling short? When He has finished measuring, He will have a complete record of the nation's moral dimensions. Then will Americans come to know the enlargement of virtue and the renovation of our shoddy permissiveness.

Prayer: *Lord, help us to care about our moral stature. Help us to seek You and exalt Your call to be a people concerned with compassion and desirous of national holiness. May we watch You measure our weaknesses. Then may we seek You and beg a return to all that made us great.* ★

PEACE TO ALL NATIONS

Rejoice greatly, O daughter of Zion!
Shout, O daughter of Jerusalem!
Behold, your King is coming to you;
He is just and having salvation,
Lowly and riding on a donkey,
A colt, the foal of a donkey.

I will cut off the chariot from Ephraim
And the horse from Jerusalem;
The battle bow shall be cut off.
He shall speak peace to the nations;
His dominion shall be "from sea to sea,
And from the River to the ends of the earth."

ZECHARIAH 9: 9-10

The peace of Christ was not given to the world to keep the world from war. It was given to remind ourselves that our very first responsibility is not to rid the world of our enemies but to get rid of the enemy that is in our hearts. We must not let anyone live in petty resentments. The rehearsal of any grudge harms

not only those we resent but ourselves as well.

Notice the depiction of the Messiah here in Zechariah. He came not on a white steed of war and conquest. No, He came riding on the foal of a donkey. There was gentleness in His demeanor. He came conquering by love, and, with love alone, He destroyed the chariots of war. He broke the killing bows of the archers. He prevented any return to weapons of hate by making sure those weapons would never be used again.

This idea of the Messiah is not one that sits well with our various theories of vengeance. After all, when we are abused by tyrants, we must fight back. Peace that will not conquer from the back of a great steed seems too anemic a reply to the great power plays of the tyrants.

But Jesus completely fulfilled this picture.

He came on the foal of a donkey, and the crowds fell down before Him crying, "Blessed is He who comes in the name of the LORD." What the Palm Sunday crowds were really saying was "Blessed is He who lays by the attire of swaggering warlords and teaches us that when old wars finish, new ones begin, and so the killing never stops and peace never comes."

Now the word "war" is ultimate. Weapons to destroy all nations lie momentarily sleeping in missile silos. We can only pray those earthen tubes will never open to send their horror abroad. How all peace-loving people long to see these great missiles uncapped and piled in rusting heaps. Then there, at the blessed place of their demise, a great Savior will once again ride on a donkey's foal. There anew the war-weary world will have to break into song, "Blessed is He who comes in the name of the Lord."

How much America has sought to break up the nuclear arsenals of the world. Sometimes her voice has come alone in the cry. But never has she given up the hope that someday all the children of the world will be able to live without this terror. The best Americans want a gentle peace for all peoples. True lovers of peace would like nothing better than for all people to beat their swords into plowshares and their spears into pruning hooks. America would like to see Zechariah's world come to be. America would like to proclaim peace to the nations and extend the rule of God from sea to sea!

Still genocide exists alongside America's intention to not let one people destroy another. Within the very center of all that's

best about America lies our determination to eradicate this worldwide fallacy: "If only I were to kill all my enemies, all that would be left to me would be friends." As long as any people see peace to be the result of having killed all their enemies, wars will go on forever. The only way to create peace is by renaming your enemies as your friends. Nobody ever goes to war against their friends. In so vast a brotherhood the word "war" could be struck from the dictionary as an antiquated term that no one any longer understood.

Prayer: *Lord, make America gentle. Make gentleness the appetite of every nation. But cleanse my life so well that I will allow myself to have no enemies and can thus say to all, "Since every person is the friend of God, the world itself is my family."* ✭

His dominion shall be

"from sea to sea,

And from the River to the

ends of the earth."

ZECHARIAH 9:10

LIGHT

You are the light of the world.
A city that is set on a hill cannot be hidden. Nor do they light a lamp and
put it under a basket, but on a lampstand, and it gives light
to all who are in the house. Let your light so shine before men, that they may
see your good works and glorify your Father in heaven.

MATTHEW 5:14–16

If the eagle is the mascot of America, light must be her symbol.

The Bible makes light its fascinating subject. God, in the beginning, said, "Let there be light!" In these simple words, God spoke into being a form of energy that blesses the universe with sight. This marvelous force called light travels at 186,000 miles per second. It reveals a rainbow of components ranging from ultraviolet to infrared. It makes visible all the wonders of God's world and brings the printed Word of God to the human eye so that it can take root in the human heart. Light is the very gift of God, given so that wonder itself is possible!

But Jesus speaks in these verses of light as proclamation. Light preaches truth. It sermonizes over eternal matters. "A city that is set on a hill cannot be hidden," said Jesus. "Nor do they light a lamp and put it under a basket." Light exists precisely to keep anything

from hiding. It exists to proclaim.

There is nothing more beautiful than taking a night walk or drive through Washington, D.C. The splendor of white monuments in focused light is most dramatic. Rejoice at architecture made brilliant: The shaft of the Washington Monument thrusting upward into the stars. The power of the Parthenon-like Lincoln temple, and its great seated patriot, looking out between those glistening columns. The Jefferson Memorial with its domed eloquence. All of these great buildings stop the eye by day, but they all but stop the heart by night. The drama is partly the product of electricity, and electricity's greatest miracle is light.

If I want to know the strength of Jesus' metaphor I have only to contrast Washington, D.C., and Beijing. When I first traveled in China the thing that captured my attention was the dim illumination of this world capital. Power is scarce and infinitely more expensive in China. To travel very far from the center of Beijing at night is to make your way mostly by headlights. To use Jesus' metaphor, I call it a great city under a bushel.

Jesus' discourse on light challenges us to let our light shine so that we can inspire the people of the entire world to live luminous

lives. As light may point up individual virtue, it should also point up national virtue. Good nations behave like good people, for they are composed of good people. These desire to copy virtue and honor righteousness, and with this goal realized the kingdom of God will be born in the intentions of good people desiring to be God's people.

P r a y e r : *Lord may our light so shine before other nations that the Christ who lives within Americans will inspire that same quality of life throughout the world. Let us learn the art of dramatic lighting by setting our focused illumination directly on You, O Christ. May we call You from darkness to reign over this needy moral night.* ★

U P O N   T H I S   R O C K   I ' L L
B U I L D   M Y   C H U R C H

And I also say to you that you are Peter,
and on this rock I will build My church, and the gates of Hades
shall not prevail against it.

M A T T H E W   1 6 : 1 8

*W*hen *Jesus established His church*, He placed a huge stumbling block in the path of tyranny. The church in time would portray the best aspects of liberty in America. It was from a church steeple that the lanterns were hung that sent Paul Revere to awake the colonists with the cry, "The British are coming!" It was a fitting signal, for church steeples have always signaled warning and change to the people of God. The inscription on Paul Revere's famous silver bowl reads,

> *To the memory of the glorious 92 members of the Honorable House of Representatives of the Massachusetts Bay, who undaunted by the insolent menaces of people in power, from a strict regard to conscience and the liberties of their constituents on the thirtieth of June 1768 voted not to rescind.*[24]

But of course it was the light from a church steeple that began the insurrection that would not cease until America had firmly

demonstrated how much liberty meant to her. There was that wonderful statement issued by the Charleston Committee of Safety: "If the British went out by water, to show two lanterns in the North Church Steeple; and if by land, one as a signal, for we were apprehensive it would be difficult to cross the Charles River or get over Boston Neck."[25]

Simply put by Longfellow, it was "One if by land, and two if by sea." Revere gave himself to steeple-watching, and determined that "I shall be ready to sound the alarm, to every Middlesex village and farm." So came the lanterns, and so the process of liberty was begun.

The great Leo Tolstoy confessed that his struggle with Christian liberty ended in a church. For years he had felt imprisoned in his sin and his need for some great reason to live. The struggle to be free in his soul was for him a dark struggle. Then at a communion service his eyes were opened. He saw the bread being broken and understood that it symbolized the body of Christ. His heart understood before his mind. He took the broken bread. Christ, the healer of broken hearts, mended his broken heart.

John Wesley confessed of a very small church at Aldersgate, "I felt my heart strangely warmed."

Martin Luther called God his Mighty Fortress but knew the earthly citadel of such a mighty God was the church of Jesus Christ.

Samuel Wesley wrote of the church that Christ was her one foundation. But he realized that the teaching of Christ on the endurance of the church meant that the church will never be vanquished. The church will endure throughout time and at the end of time will still be clearly in place.

Mid toil and tribulation and tumult of her war,
She waits the consummation of peace forevermore;
Till with the vision glorious, her longing eyes are blest,
And the great church victorious will be the church at rest.

P r a y e r : *Lord, may the steeples of America's churches ever be the place Americans look to discover liberty. May we see Your words to Your apostles as the heralds of all things free. May we never forget that on a singular day You had founded Your church so securely that the gates of hell would never prevail against it. Now may the endurance of that church stand for what is dearest and best in the freedom all people should have to call Christ Lord.* ✶

BIG STICKS
AND LARGER GRACE

Then Jesus said to him,
"Put your sword in its place, for all who take the sword
will perish by the sword."

MATTHEW 26:52

America has reluctantly entered most foreign wars. This is partly because she had the luxury of wide oceans on either side of her to make her feel safe. But it may even more be the result of her nonaggressive status toward making any other nation her own personal booty. She wants to own no land if that land must be taken from those who live there.

Her greatest of anthems speaks of her reluctance to conquer:

When conquer we must, when our cause it is just,
Let this be our motto in God is our trust.

Oh, if only Napoleon could have sung those words. Or Tamerlane. Or Genghis Khan. What if Kaiser Bill or Adolf had been willing to say, "We will conquer only when we must, when our cause it is just." Alas, it was Le Pouge who remarked that if all the wars in the world in the past seven hundred years were put together they would

fuel a fountain of blood, running seven hundred liters an hour since the beginning of written world history.

Americans didn't want to control or own Germany, whereas Germany, twice in the American Century, tried to own everyone else. Americans seem to realize the truth in Christ's saying, "Put your sword in its place, for all who take the sword will perish by the sword." But even if we don't die by it, to kill other people and take what is theirs grates all that is hidden in the heart of America.

Theodore Roosevelt said, "Speak softly, but carry a big stick." There is something uncanny in the statement. Wars have never been won with sticks. Sticks are what you grab in the face of sudden aggression to defend yourself. They are not the weapons of advance.

America has reluctantly taken up the sword, only when the stick was no longer able to guarantee freedom to the world. Liberty was always the prize. If it can be guaranteed by stick, sticks are enough. If not, the all-important treasure of free peoples everywhere should be defended.

This has often been done at great price.

Between 1941 and 1944, my four older sisters each in turn married servicemen, and our family, like so many in those years, knew the

agony of giving of our own to bring the world to peace. Only one of the four never returned, but the suffering was not partial—the whole of a family hurts when any part of it is lost. While my brother-in-law was killed in occupied Japan immediately after the war was over, the grief it brought to our family was a reminder that war seems to go on killing even when it is over. Perhaps that's what Jesus was trying to say to His disciples in Gethsemane. Swords are never a long-time solution to national unhappiness. It is rarely possible to kill our way to peace.

"When conquer we must, when our cause it is just"—well then, maybe we will go to war. But those who are too eager to wield the sword need to be reminded by Jesus that they may someday die by it.

Prayer: *Lord, help us to proclaim no unholy "holy wars." Help us never to take other people's freedom, to never forget that what we hold dearest in our own hearts is dearest to others too. May we cherish above all the right to pray and hold all matters of conscience sacred to You. Teach us that national liberty is most treasured by those of us who, in trusting and loving Christ, have discovered Your inner liberty.* ✶

Light,
America's Best Export

Then Jesus came and spoke to them saying,
"All authority has been given to Me in heaven and on earth. Go therefore
and make disciples of all the nations, baptizing them in the name
of the Father and of the Son and of the Holy Spirit, teaching them to observe
all things that I have commanded you; and lo, I am with you always,
even to the end of age." Amen.

MATTHEW 28:18–20

In 1620, the Puritans landed at Plymouth Rock. They came for the sake of their conscience, and since they were the first white colonists in that area, there was borne in their resolve the idea that in New England faith had found a safe place to rehearse its truths.

But it would not be long before the nation would grow up thousands of churches and dozens of denominations. Christian missions was soon to become a major export of American Christians.

Early in the eighteenth century, Isaac Watts had written their anthem of advance:

Jesus shall reign where'er the sun, does his successive journeys run;
His Kingdom spread from shore to shore, till moons shall wax and
wane no more.

From north to south the princes meet, to pay their homage at his feet;
While western empires own their lord, and savage tribes attend his word.
People and realms of ev'ry tongue, dwell on his love with sweetest song,
And infant voices shall proclaim their early blessings on his name.

From the burgeoning new denominations of the eighteenth and nineteenth centuries, good Americans went to take the gospel of Christ around the world. They were not trying to be American missionaries, adopting a red, white, and blue Jesus in some double attempt to "Americanize" while they "Christianized" the planet. But in their minds they were aware that America's greatness lay in the fact that she was rooted in values that came directly from the Bible.

The American missionaries did Christianize the world. They conquered in the name of love. But in addition to making converts, they made better medicine, better education, and better lives wherever they preached the lofty gospel. Of course, back home in America, they were the brunt of multicultural criticisms. "Other cultures have a right to keep their own religions and their own way of life without being challenged to become Christians!" cried some. "Christian mission is a way of subjugating other people's religious freedom by insisting they

become Christians!" cried others.

Thus missionaries became the unsung heroes of America. Under heavy intellectual fire they planted churches and raised schools and hospitals around the world. Bit by bit, however, they did awaken a worldwide craving for liberty. Those nations where they took Christ would in the passing of years cry out to become as politically free as the missionaries were free in America. Revolutions rose as autocrats were deposed. Revolutions are rarely kind or seasoned with mercy. The message of the Cross has always awakened a love of freedom. It did in America and it has around the world.

Prayer: *Lord, help us to obey You in taking Your gospel around the world. Help us never to paint You with American colors. You stand above any mere national idol. Help us also to realize that spiritual freedom and civic liberty both are ideas rooted in Your gospel.* ★

The Refreshing Center
of All Liberty

The Spirit of the LORD *is upon Me,*
Because He has anointed Me
To preach the gospel to the poor;
He has sent Me to heal the brokenhearted,
To proclaim liberty to the captives
And recovery of sight to the blind,
To set at liberty those who are oppressed;
To proclaim the acceptable year of the LORD.

LUKE 4:18–19

One of Christianity's greatest hymn writers, William Cowper, wrote in 1771,

There is a fountain filled with blood,
Drawn from Emmanuel's veins,
And sinners plunged beneath that flood
Lose all their guilty stains.

There has always existed the notion that when we are freed from sin we are free indeed.

No nation is more seriously enslaved than that which loses

its moral conscience.

When Jesus went home to preach in Nazareth, He stood among the Nazarenes, His hometown family and friends, and reminded them that when the Messiah came He would be in the liberation business. The Nazarenes were not ready to accept this Jesus, whom they knew too well, as the Liberator.

But Jesus understood that no one can ever be free who is immoral. So at the front of His great kingdom was an invitation to all believers to confess their sins and unshackle their souls.

In an 1815 decision, the Supreme Court ruled,

The destruction of morality renders the power of the government invalid. The corruption of the public mind, in general, and debauching the manners of youth, in particular, by lewd and obscene pictures exhibited to view, must necessarily be attended with the most injurious consequences . . . No man is permitted to corrupt the morals of the people.[26]

Now the invitation passes on to the nation. We are often told that we live in an age that has been liberated from the whole idea of sin. Sin, some say, is an old-fashioned idea, and

guilt is completely unnecessary to those who will simply say sin doesn't exist.

But denial doesn't eradicate sin. It is an addiction. There are none so blind as those who agree that sight is unnecessary. Virtue only belongs to the honest. It is always right to shed self-righteousness and ask God for moral cleansing.

So let us seek the refreshing fountains of God. Let us be altogether clean. Let us belong to the light and shun the darkness. Then will our liberty be free—truly free—from the idolatry of our indulgence.

Prayer: *Lord, make our entire nation clean and begin the cleansing in my heart first. Teach me that those who hunger and thirst after righteousness are free and their appetite preserves their liberty.* ★

YOU SHALL KNOW
THE TRUTH
AND THE TRUTH SHALL
MAKE YOU FREE

And you shall know the truth, and the truth shall make you free.

JOHN 8:32

It was such an unworkable philosophy, we are amazed we didn't see it before. We now know we never needed to fear communism. Communism declared there was no God and then set out to build a great society of equality on such an obvious lie.

So for the middle seven decades of the twentieth century we slept in fear. But what was it we feared? We feared a huge threat based on a huge lie. The lie produced slavery. Two-thirds of the world's population fell under the sway of the red star. Millions died, and millions more knew the chains of slavery.

Then bit by bit the walls came down. Berlin first, then the Balkans disintegrated. Religion reclaimed the Caribbean. Statues of those who taught their people there was no God toppled and fell across Europe.

Why? Because the world understood that lies imprison us.

Truth sets us free.

Is it any wonder that Lincoln said, "Four score and seven years ago our forefathers brought forth a new nation, conceived in Liberty and

dedicated to the proposition that all men are created equal."

If Lenin's lie disintegrated in seventy years, look what Lincoln's truth did in but a few more. Because of Lincoln's truth, slaves were freed and a nation was restored to unity. Then when all Americans were free, the truth that set them free captured the imagination—yes, even the hearts—of the world.

God reached out in Christ to say, "Come to Me, all you who labor and are heavy laden, and I will give you rest" (Matt. 11:28). Truth serves all a generous portion of liberty. So it was that Paul the apostle said, "There is neither Jew nor Greek, there is neither slave nor free, there is neither male nor female; for you are all one in Christ Jesus" (Gal. 3:28).

Truth alone produces such liberty as this.

America is first among all nations in championing this truth.

David Ramsay, a member of the Continental Congress, wrote:

Had I a voice that could be heard from New Hampshire to Georgia, it should be exerted in urging the necessity of disseminating virtue and knowledge among our citizens. On this subject, the policy of the eastern States is well worthy of imitation. The wise people of that extremity of the union never form a new township without making arrangments that secure to its inhabitants the instruction of youth and the public preaching of the gospel. Hence their children are taught to know their rights and to respect themselves. They grow up good members of the society and staunch defenders of their country's cause.[27]

When people know the truth it sets them free. When they live the truth it sets the next generation free. To know the truth guarantees today; to live the truth guarantees forever.

P r a y e r : *God, help us to tell Your truth. But more than that help us to be ready to live this truth. For the world has had her share of lies and slavery. In Christ we hold the reply to all falsehood. The truth sets us free. Our freedom is evidence we have true liberty.* ★

BREAD FROM THE LARDER
OF GOD

Repay no one evil for evil. Have regard for good things
in the sight of all men. If it is possible, as much as depends on you, live
peaceably with all men. Beloved, do not avenge yourselves, but
rather give place to wrath; for it is written, "Vengeance is Mine, I will
repay," says the Lord.
Therefore "If your enemy is hungry, feed him;
If he is thirsty, give him a drink;
For in so doing you will heap coals of fire on his head."
Do not be overcome by evil, but overcome evil with good.

ROMANS 12:17–21

America is the servant of Him who took bread and blessed it and divided it among the thousands. There is an old tale popularly circulated among revivalists and campground meetings that tells of a little boy who supplied the bread that day that Jesus divided the loaves. At first the lad felt great pride as he watched Christ breaking the bread that had been his lunch. It was he who, according to the Scriptures, had given his lunch to Jesus. It was a simple lunch of five loaves and two fishes.

As Jesus successfully broke bread and passed out the fish, the child, realizing that Jesus had broken his lunch, kept repeating over and

over, "That's my bread, that's my fish." But the further Jesus multiplied his little lunch, the more honesty owned the day. At last, as the boy saw thousands devouring his lunch, he had to admit, "That's not my bread, that's not my fish anymore."

Americans have thanked God for His abundance, but they have always been forced to admit that the loaves God gives are not our bread but His. From year to year, decade to decade, American has pinched from her abundance and distributed it to the needy world.

If our enemies are hungry we are to feed them. This became our reason when many of the former communist countries were forced to admit their economic failures. Then America felt it was important not to remember that these were once our enemies with the nuclear capability to destroy us.

Now it was not our bread.

Now it was not our fish.

It was God's.

New England Colonials were so in love with God's providence that they gave a small town in Rhode Island the name. In the ensuing years it was to become a great city. Now its lengthy name sticks out into the blue Atlantic on the map. Different than many colonial towns,

the very name is a Christian doctrine. It is a theological word of relationship. God who owns all is in the business of providing us with His good gifts. From prison the apostle Paul wrote a letter to the Philippians, and a single line from that gallant and loving letter is a promise of providence: "My God shall supply all your need according to His riches in glory by Christ Jesus."

Paul's commandment to feed our enemies is to teach us not so much the art of charity but the art of widening our definitions. Are we to divide the world into our friends and our enemies? Certainly not. We are to love our friends and redefine our enemies as friends. Thus Americans prepare the table and call to all the world's hungry, "Come, eat, dear friends, and blessed former enemies for we are all debtors to the goodness of God. Your hunger and ours know a common provider. Let us praise with thanksgiving the Great Meeter of our every need."

P r a y e r : *Lord, help generosity to mark our spirit, for if we will not be generous we can never be like Christ. May we feed our enemies in the name of that same grace that ended our enmity with You. We are Your friends and thus call the world to the wider circle of Your friendship.* ★

A L L   N A T I O N S   W I L L   C O M E
A N D   W O R S H I P

They sing the song of Moses, the servant of God,
and the song of the Lamb, saying:
"Great and marvelous are Your works,
Lord God Almighty!
Just and true are Your ways,
O King of the saints!
Who shall not fear You, O Lord, and glorify Your name?
For You alone are holy.
For all nations shall come and worship before You,
For Your judgments have been manifested."

R E V E L A T I O N   1 5 : 3 – 4

Beneath the massive orange cables of the Golden
Gate Bridge they came. Most of them didn't come because they
were seeking to worship the God of a great nation. They came
because that nation beckoned them toward a common liberty
that held an uncommon promise.

America was a place to be free—free to live and grow and
pursue a dream of having a free family and a piece of life that
offered a home and enough to eat.

But having arrived in the New World they met her citizens,

and many of them were convinced that great nations do not just happen where the thousand immigrants assemble. Great nations occur where God touches the earth with promise and the human heart with hope. Where promise and hope meet, patriotism is born.

In concluding his famous cemetery speech at Gettysburg, Lincoln reminded us all of the great appeal of America:

> *It is rather for us to be here dedicated to the great task remaining before us, that from these honored dead we take increased devotion to that cause to which they gave the last full measure of devotion—that we here highly resolve that these dead shall not have died in vain—that this nation, under God, shall have a new birth of freedom, and that the government of the people, by the people, and for the people shall not perish from the earth.*[28]

Lincoln died before he could fully understand the magnificent appeal of the truth behind Gettysburg. This nation was to become for all nations what the Gettysburg address so enticingly held out to the disenfranchised of the world. America